CALM THE F*CK DOWN!

A Covid Bedtime Story

ISBN: 978-0-578-80620-4

CTFD, LLC
C/O Jokar Productions, LLC, Redondo Beach, CA 90277
www.calmthefdown.us

CALM THE FUCK DOWN!

A COVID BEDTIME STORY

by Ivana B. Dunne

Illustrated by Walter Carzon Studio

Covid is making you anxious.
In your worries you feel you might drown.
For sleep read this chill bedtime story
To help you to calm the fuck down.

When Amazon wasn't fulfilling
And you were just waiting around
For the bleach and the hand sanitizer
You freaked out. But now calm the fuck down.

Your neighbor bought all of the T.P.
And then there was none to be found.
What's with the hoarding? (Such assholes.)
Take deep breaths and then calm the fuck down.

Your hands are still raw from the washing
And we've all gained a few extra pounds.
I hope you're not still washing groceries.
Just eat 'em and calm the fuck down.

Dr. Fauci knows all of the research.
Dr. Birx has done all of the rounds.
Don't inject or ingest disinfectant.
Wear a mask and just calm the fuck down.

You feel like your throat has a tickle.
Normal temp but your fear is profound.
It's the fifth time this month, just get real now
You're fine! (Ugh.) Now calm the fuck down.

Your friends in New York don't have cooties.
Yes, they live in 'the Big Apple' town.
But they quarantined too (and are safer than you).
So relax and just calm the fuck down.

THANK YOU OUR LOCAL HEROES

You Zoom with your family and book club.
In your sweatpants, you look like a clown.
Before you commit hara-kiri,
Make a phone call and calm the fuck down.

There's a place far away you must get to.
You won't fly 'cause you're too tightly wound.
Wearing diapers, you pack up the cooler—that's wack!
OMG, will you calm the fuck down?

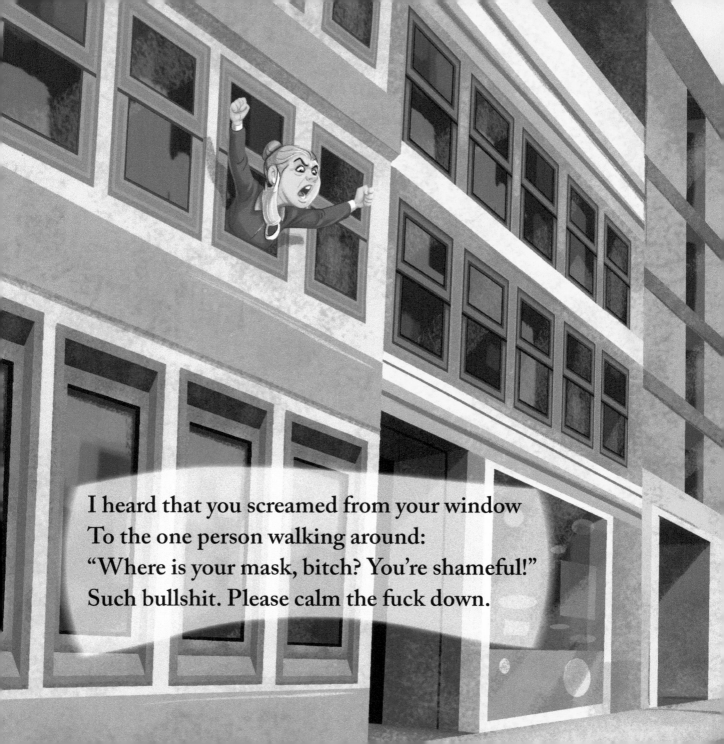

I heard that you screamed from your window
To the one person walking around:
"Where is your mask, bitch? You're shameful!"
Such bullshit. Please calm the fuck down.

Your kids want your help during homeschool.
(All the adjectives, adverbs, and nouns . . .)
Can't remember that shit and you're working.
Accept failure and calm the fuck down.

You thought you got rid of your daughter
Who was safely ensconced out at Brown.
She's back and she's driving you crazy.
Try yoga and calm the fuck down.

Pre-pandemic, your marriage was working.
But your spouse is now always around.
Yes, it's sucky but what are your options?
Have a cocktail and calm the fuck down.

They say the vaccine is effective.
So there's really no reason to frown.
Say goodnight to the moon and your sweetheart.
Go to sleep now. And calm the fuck down.

ABOUT THE AUTHOR

IVANA B. DUNNE graduated from MI School of Sleep Hygiene and OR Rhyming School for Non-Rhymers. She became inspired to write picture books in verse after years of bedtime-reading to her bewildered neighbors. Now she gets story ideas from her condo association. Her award-winning poetry has been read at the Pandemic Day-Drinkers Book Club, where she received their highest award for poetry: a half-bottle of chardonnay. When she isn't writing, she loves re-counting her toilet paper rolls in case she counted wrong the first time. She lives with her life partner, condo association board president U.R. McNutty.

ABOUT THE ILLUSTRATOR

WALTER CARZON is an Argentinian freelance artist who designs illustrations, characters, and comics. His team at Walter Carzon Studio offers creative services for publishing projects, merchandizing, and advertising.

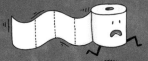

CPSIA information can be obtained
at www.ICGtesting.com
Printed in the USA
BVHW022250090122
625857BV00005B/26

9 780578 806204